Endorsements

Dr. Joan Bragar is a world-class myth-buster. In this delightfully compelling read, you're going to find out why finding happy, healthy love is not only possible, but probable when you follow her simple and easy-to-follow protocol.

- Katherine Woodward
New York Times *bestselling author*

I found Joan's book sincere and heartfelt. She was remarkably vulnerable in her telling of her own experiences. It makes it feel possible and even a little exciting to find love in my fifties!

—Saleswoman raising children on her own, eager to find love.

If you are like me, wanting to find love late in life and not sure how or too afraid because of the fear of getting hurt again, this is a must-read. And even better, besides reading the book, reach out to Joan to get her personal coaching to support you to find the love you have always dreamt of.

—Scientist with a successful career who
w

I found just the man for me in so many ways. I wanted to thank you for all your love and support and concur that love is possible after 50! He just wants to take care of me and have fun outdoors and that's what I wanted! All he needs from me is my love.

—Hospice nurse dedicated to supporting others,
who wanted support in her own life

Never Too Late for Love is a gem and valuable at any stage of one's life and honestly at any age! Being an Internet dating newbie, it allowed me a better understanding and gave me more courage to continue on my path of finding my "One"!

—Grandmother who wants to
"stay in the game" of life and love

Never Too Late for Love is detailed but not too wordy, with specific guidelines to follow, and personal enough to make readers feel they are having an intimate conversation with a good friend.

—Lawyer who wants to find a man
who is thrilled that she is successful

Never Too Late for Love

Never Too Late *for* Love!

The Successful Woman's Guide to Online Dating in the Second Half of Life

JOAN BRAGAR, EdD

NEW YORK

LONDON • NASHVILLE • MELBOURNE • VANCOUVER

Never Too Late for Love

The Successful Woman's Guide to Online Dating
in the Second Half of Life

Throughout this book there are examples from client's lives. To ensure privacy their names and some of the details of their experiences have been changed. The personal examples from my own life have not been altered.

Published in New York, New York, by Morgan James Publishing in partnership with Difference Press. Morgan James is a trademark of Morgan James, LLC.
www.MorganJamesPublishing.com

ISBN 9781642797923 paperback
ISBN 9781642797930 eBook
ISBN 9781642797947 audio
Library of Congress Control Number: 2019949861

Cover Design: Jennifer Stimson

Interior Design: Chris Treccani   www.3dogcreative.net

Editor: Moriah Howell

Book Coaching: The Author Incubator

Morgan James is a proud partner of Habitat for Humanity Peninsula and Greater Williamsburg. Partners in building since 2006.

Get involved today! Visit
MorganJamesPublishing.com/giving-back

*This book is dedicated to the
women and men of my generation,
who are pioneering new ways to love.*

Table of Contents

Foreword

I'm old enough to remember when being older than 50 was... well, old. Happily, those days are long gone. Today, due in large part to the wonders of hormone therapies, longer lifespans and changing social mores, so that there are now more people over 50 who are divorced than widowed, "Silver Seekers" have become the fastest-growing demographic in the on-line dating world.

Yet as quickly as culture is changing, when it comes to finding love in the second half of life, some things have been far too slow to evolve. For one, the myth that we have to have a lean, cellulite-free bodies for a man to be attracted to us. Or two, that men prefer women who are younger and less successful than they are. Or three, that there are no good (or conscious) men out there who would be worth our while.

Dr. Joan Bragar is a world-class myth-buster. In this delightfully compelling read, you're going to find out why finding happy, healthy love is not only possible, but probable when you follow her simple and easy-to-follow protocol. In her grounded, practical, insightful, and visionary way, she offers a step-by-step blueprint for how to create a future of deep happiness in love, no matter how many disappointments you may have experienced in your past.

Dr. Joan is a woman that I myself look to for advice. I'm thrilled to now share her with you so that she can bless your life with as much infectious inspiration, clarity, and empowerment as she's given me over the years.

– Katherine Woodward Thomas
New York Times Bestselling author of
Calling in "The One" and *Conscious Uncoupling*

Introduction:

Do You Want
Love in Your Life?

I was fifty-seven when my marriage ended. I had a successful career and wonderful grown children, but I still wanted to be in a committed relationship with a man. I was worried that I was getting older. Would men still find me attractive? Would I have the stamina for the inevitable disappointments of online dating? I didn't know any other way to find the love I was looking for, so I reached out for the best coaching support I could find.

This book is for the woman who has succeeded on her own terms. You are proud of your accomplishments, but still find that something is missing in your personal life.

You may have had loving relationships, but at this point in life you feel that it might be good to have a committed partner. You have been unable to find him and secretly fear that you just don't know what it takes to have a great man who is committed to caring for you.

You have succeeded in work. Now you want to be successful in love. Like me, you may have learned by now that having "smarts" does not ensure relationship success. And if you are in the second half of life, you may be increasingly worried about whether this kind of love is still available to you.

In my work as a leadership consultant, I support accomplished people to get the results they most want in their work and their personal lives. I see a persistent pattern among successful women; many are giving their all to make important contributions to others, but going home at night exhausted and alone.

Being Single

You are not unusual if you are single in the United States. Close to half of sixty-year-old women in the U.S. are single – some due to widowhood, but an unprecedented number because of divorce or the decision to remain single.

The anthropologist Katherine Bateson, in her book *Composing a Further Life, The Age of Active Wisdom*, documented the impact of our increased life spans. There is now the possibility of added years of health when you are no longer concerned with child raising or career success – a time when you are free, perhaps for the first time, to pursue a life you truly love.

In this phase of life, you are wiser and more accepting of yourself. You feel proud of your accomplishments and the contributions you have made. These could be the best years of your life. Living a longer life doesn't necessarily mean more years of infirmity at the end; instead, it means the possibility of more years of active living. That is why many women are divorcing after long marriages – they don't want to live thirty more years in a relationship that has died.

My fellow leadership consultant, Avivah Wittenberg Cox, author of *Late Love – Mating in Maturity*, says there is "An explosion of 'grey' divorce and remarriage in the over-50s. With children departing into their own journeys and ever-longer lives stretching out ahead, more mature adults are leaping, unconventionally and aspirationally, at a last chance at love."

The question is: *Would you be happier with a good man in your life?*

Having a Man in Your Life – Is It Worth It?

Having a man in is not a necessity. It is possible to fill your life with family, friends, and activities that contribute to your sense of wholeness and wellbeing.

But returning home to an empty house, and an empty bed, can make the night too long and too lonely for many of us. I know. I've been there.

I was fifty-seven I when I divorced after a ten-year marriage. I knew that I wanted to be in relationship with a man again, but I had many doubts and fears:

Would men still find me attractive?

Would I be able to find a man who was single and sane?

How would I venture into the unknown world of online dating?

You may also be concerned about taking on the role of caretaker at this stage of life. That is not inevitable. Successful women do not necessarily need to take this role in a relationship.

Many of my clients and friends (and my daughter) are in relationships with men who are happy to take a lead role in support. These men have their own interests and pursuits in life, but taking care of their loved ones is a priority for them. These empowered men have the self-esteem to support women in their aspirations. My husband is one these great men.

Talking About Our Generation...

In Punta Gorda, Florida, the town where my husband and I live in the winter, you see couples in their fifties, sixties, seventies and eighties who are healthy and living active lives. Large numbers of these "boomers" are active in new enterprises and community causes. We are not going "quietly into the night!"

We are among the first generations for whom marriage and family were not mandated by society. Women are capable of building and sustaining friendships that fill many needs. However, I believe that as primates there is a "limbic" attachment that we get from a partner who sleeps with us at night and cares for us during the day.

In *A General Theory of Love*, Lewis, Amini and Lannon define the term "limbic resonance" as a "mutual and internal adaptation whereby two mammals become attuned to each other's inner states." When we are close to an attentive partner, our heart rate, respiration, and blood pressure change to correspond to theirs, and we are soothed in essential ways.

Does this mean that we should partner with anyone or stay in relationships when they are no longer serving us? No; that is the bondage that previous generations were forced to live in. When women did not have civil rights or access to education and paid work, they were unable to freely choose (or choose to leave) their mates.

We are not looking to go back to the times when marriage was a form of conscription, or even to the more recent period when it was assumed that marriages should last until death – *though this is still the image of marriage most of us carry in our minds.* The truth is, as Margaret Mead predicted more than a half century ago, that the predominant form of mating has become "*serial monogamy*" – committed relationships that may not last an entire lifetime.

This enormous change is the result of our greater freedom of choice.

Men and women in the West, for the most part, no longer need to be in marriages that are determined by locked-in gender roles and expectations, whereas in traditional cultures, marriage is an economic exchange of activities that are essential for living. Today, men can get food (and sex) without marriage, and women can support themselves financially (and have sex) without being legally tied to a man.

In her book *Committed*, Elizabeth Gilbert (author of *Eat, Pray, Love*) interviewed people around the world to learn what marriage meant to them.

In a primitive rice-growing community in South East Asia, she asked the women how they chose a husband. The women laughed and said, "What? They are all the same!" This is how marriage can be viewed when gender roles are rigidly prescribed.

But for our generation of women in the West, enormous shifts have occurred in our lifetime. If we were fortunate enough to come from families who could encourage and support us, we were among the first women who have had access to higher education and professional training.

More importantly, we were the first generation of women to benefit from widespread access to birth control. Starting in 1960, the "pill" made early marriage and childbearing a choice – no longer a necessity or a cultural norm. Birth control was the real revolution of the twentieth century, giving women other options besides a lifetime of only caring for family and home.

These new ways of relating opened up possibilities and opportunities that were expansive for many. I, for one, have had a life of many rich opportunities.

I've been a student at Harvard, a community and labor organizer, an organizational consultant, and I've taught leadership in health ministries and universities around the world. I now coach people who want more happiness in love and work.

But this life of many choices was not without its costs.

Finding Love

As I pivoted into each new chapter, I oftentimes found that the man that I was with was not necessarily going with me. He had his own direction and priorities in life, and they didn't always align with mine.

The absence of fixed roles opens up exciting possibilities for both genders. But it also creates dilemmas that we are only now learning how to address.

At the end of my fifties, my ten-year marriage to an Egyptian doctor that had taken me around the world teaching leadership in health systems in Egypt, Afghanistan, and many countries across Africa, came to an end. Our whirlwind global romance and marriage had not withstood domesticity in the U.S.

When I found myself divorcing, again, at age fifty-seven, I was scared.

I didn't know anything about online dating, and I wanted to learn how to find and choose a man who would support me in my current phase of life.

To face this challenge, I engaged a world-class coach, the family therapist, Katherine Woodward Thomas, author of the bestselling books, *Calling in "The One"* and *Conscious Uncoupling*. Katherine was my mentor and coach as I learned how to find happy healthy love.

I learned a great deal in the process of dating forty men over two years. (Mark Twain says that you can learn something holding a cat by the tail that you can't learn any other way!) I had to get past my fears and doubts to arrive at the happy life I now have with my husband. These experiences formed the backdrop for my research into the practices for finding love in the second half of life.

I got so committed to learning how to achieve breakthroughs in love and relationships that I became certified by Katherine as a *Calling in "The One"* and *Conscious Uncoupling Coach*, adding these offerings to my leadership coaching.

Learning the Practices That Lead to Love

I have spent a lifetime studying (and teaching) the practices that empower people to get the results they most care about. I have used these practices, based on my original doctoral research at Harvard, to design leadership development programs that I delivered around the world. These practices are documented in my book, *Leading for Results: Five Practices to Use in Your Personal and Professional Life*.

But being single late in life was one of the greatest challenges I have faced. There were no clear signposts to mark the path forward. The practices I had to learn to face this challenge were unique.

I met my husband Marc just before my sixtieth birthday. He had had his own share of adventures (and children) and was excited to meet someone who was smart and adventurous. (By the way, smart men like smart women, so you can't use being smart as an excuse for not finding your mate!)

This book is a message of hope from me to you. I am going to share with you what I had to learn (and what you *can* learn) and what I had to do (and what you *can* do) to find love in your life. I've included reflection questions and exercises that I use with my coaching clients. My hope is that you will use these to get the result you most care about – a loving and committed life partner.

Finding a partner later in life poses challenges that you may not be prepared for. This book is a guide to help you navigate the dilemmas of online dating so that you *can* find the love you want in your life.

If this were an easy process, then everyone would be doing it. What is easy is to get discouraged and quit. I'm not going to let you do that, because the reward at the end is too great to miss. It is the fullness of a life lived in love.

You have been able to learn what you needed to move your career forward. Now, learn what you need to do to bring lasting love into your life!

"Our inquiry on love and relationship has been much more challenging for me than any of the scientific inquiries

I have encountered. Love and relationship cannot be quantified or calculated with some algorithm in order to maximize the output. That's what makes us human. I am very grateful for your coaching to help me becoming more connected with my own feelings and building skills to be connected with others at a deeper level."

Director-Level Scientist,
Calling in "The One" coaching client

To learn more about my coaching, visit www.joanbragar.com

How Can We "Have It All" at This Stage of Our Lives?

"You have a right to a career and a family."
– Ellie Bragar, 1968

M y mother, Ellie Bragar, was raised by a single mother in Brooklyn. She had always longed to go to college, but needed to work in the garment district in Manhattan to support her mother. She didn't get to college until age thirty-two, with help from my father. When she was forty-two I attended her college graduation. She wept through the entire ceremony. At age eleven I had no idea why she was weeping. Now I understand what it took for her, as a woman of her generation, to manifest her dreams.

My mother always told me, "You have a right to a career and a family." I'm starting to understand what she meant by this when I speak with many women who say they've gotten the message that success in their career is their first priority. Unlike previous generations, starting a family is oftentimes not at the top of their list. The opportunities that our generation fought so hard for may have inadvertently derailed many women from having love in their lives.

Many of us have married and had children. And that worked out for as long as it did. If you are reading this book, I'm guessing your marriage didn't last forever. You may have had many relationships in your adult life, some of which were marriages and others that were not. Women of our generation have found a wide variety of ways to approach the relationship options that were given us.

Marc and I feel that these are the best years of our lives. But the reward of living them with someone we love was something we both had to work hard for. He was on online dating sites for eight years. I was on them for two. We both have our share of stories about the people we met!

Below are the practices that supported me to persevere to find love. I will briefly describe them here, and then will provide more detail on how to implement them in the following chapters.

Practice One: Clarify Your Intention

Be clear about the kind of relationship you are intending to create, and return to your intention when you face setbacks in dating. By sharing these intentions with a committed listener or coach, you sustain yourself on the path to getting the love you deserve.

Practice Two: Envision Love Fulfilled

If you want to have love in your life, you begin by living a life of love. Do this in your heart, in your home, and in your relationships with others. Be the loving experience that you want to have, so that you are ready with a loving heart and home when the right man appears.

Practice Three: Learn How to Date Online

Setting up a profile, getting the right photos, learning how to reach out to, and how to respond to, men online are all new skills for most of us. The very nature of dating has changed. You will need to learn how to date effectively.

Practice Four: Know How to Deal with the Disappointments of Dating

Disappointments are inevitable in dating. Each disappointment can trigger old hurt parts of ourselves. Too often, the consequence is that we stop reaching out to meet new people. It is important to learn how to move through these setbacks so that you can continue to meet eligible men.

Practice Five: Open Your Life to Having a (Real) Man

My husband and I, after reading each other's online profiles, were both skeptical if we were a match for each other. But we were willing to take a chance. What a surprise to learn that he was a wonderful man… who would be my future husband. This practice shows you how to become open to having real men show up in your life.

Getting Support

These practices are simple, but not easy. You don't have to do these on your own – that's why I'm here! Each practice will be explained fully so that you will have the confidence you need to venture forth successfully into the world of online dating.

The first thing I did after my divorce… well the first thing I did after my divorce was to sit in my house for a year and enjoy the feeling of not being in an unhappy marriage. But after that year I realized that time was wasting, that I was not getting any younger. This fact alone motivated me to learn how to date online.

I reached out for support to Katherine Woodward Thomas, author of *Calling in "The One,"* the book that has changed thousands of lives. I read her book, took her online classes, and one day during a class when she said there was one spot available to do private coaching with her, I shot off an email to her immediately – before she was finished speaking. I was determined to get that spot.

I paid Katherine more than what a trip to Portugal would have cost – more than I had ever paid any coach or therapist. I did this because I was really clear that the task in front of me was monumental, and that without masterful help I might not succeed. I knew I needed the best help in the world. I was also clear that the benefits of going on a one-time trip to Portugal would be nowhere near the benefits of finding a man I loved, who loved me back!

The first thing Katherine and I did in our coaching was to set a clear intention for what I wanted. I intended to call a great man into my life by my fifty-ninth birthday.

Well, guess what happened? At fifty-nine, after dating several men, I was still single. What else could I do but set my intention again? I intended that I would call in a great man by age sixty. This focused intention was critical to my ongoing efforts and eventual success.

I was starting to get to my wits' end when, just months before my sixtieth birthday, yet another three-date "relationship" fizzled. It was only my intention, that I had spoken aloud to my coach and committed to, that kept me going.

As part of my coaching, I learned to examine my core beliefs about love. Reflecting on early experiences in my family, including my own parents' divorce, I saw that I had made decisions as a young girl, including, "I am on my own" and that "Men cannot be trusted."

These beliefs led me to choose men who were smart but not committed to taking care of me. I needed to uplevel those beliefs if I wanted to call in a caring husband.

I claimed the deeper truth of my adult life, that, "*I am deeply connected to others and others are deeply connected to me.*" Wow – life showed up differently when I saw at it from this perspective.

I began to live my life differently as new possibilities showed up. I started to schedule annual family vacations with my brother and my grown children and their families – a tradition that has continued for years.

I planned a party for my sixtieth birthday to which I invited everyone who was important in my life. It was incredibly heartwarming. My son traveled from California and my brother came from Holland to celebrate. I had people there from every decade of my life.

It was into this atmosphere of love that Marc showed up. We had only been on four dates when I invited him to my birthday party. I wasn't sure where the relationship was going, but I knew that I liked him. It turned out that my friends and family liked him as well.

Jumping ahead, Marc and I are now best friends (and snuggle buddies) who enjoy living a full life together. We stay in to have fun and we go out to have fun. We eat together, shop for food together, and share a home together – the things that are the joys of life. We also go to the gym, walk, bicycle, go to yoga, and bring friends into our shared life. We are there for each other in all of life's ups and downs.

We share seven adult children – ranging in ages from twenty-six to forty-six. They give us a great deal of pleasure as we watch their lives unfold. I want you to have this gift to love and be loved by a man who cares for your family as his own.

Alone Again

In our generation now there are now unprecedented numbers of people living alone. At our condo building in Boston, there are more men and women living alone than people living in couples. And there are thousands of sixty-year-olds on Match.com in the Boston area (I know that from my personal experience!). Loneliness is a now seen as a major public health crisis. When people do not have significant attachments, loneliness can be detrimental to health.

Society has not caught up with the needs of our generation. Fifty years after the "Summer of Love," we find ourselves confused and uncertain about how to find love. Many have given up. *But how can you give up on love?*

There are few mixers for people in our generation. Traditional matchmakers are not available to most of us. But there are online sites that are beginning to address our issues. And there is a growing body of knowledge about how to effectively meet people using these sites. The practices in this book will show you how to succeed at this daunting challenge.

A Dream Come True

I am working from our home in Florida. When we look out our windows, we see the blue water of Charlotte Harbor with white boats in the distance, and green mangroves that line the shore. We watch beautiful sunsets from our porch every night.

We first imagined this place on a "Vision Board" that Marc and I created together in the first few months of our relationship. I wanted to see what Marc saw in his future so I asked him if he wanted to make a board with me. Among other things, we both found and pasted pictures of homes on winding rivers. Lo and behold, we now live at the mouth of the Peace River. We actually imagined ourselves here. I will give instructions on how to create your own Vision Board.

Moving from Our Vision to a Beautiful Life Together

It took me awhile to begin to know that Marc was the trustworthy man who defied my childhood belief that "men couldn't be trusted." I took two years to get to know him in a variety of situations before committing to marriage.

We married at Boston City Hall in a sweet ceremony with a Justice of Peace. Later that year, we celebrated our marriage with our families on Cape Cod in a beachfront wedding.

Shortly after we married, we went to Florida for a week's vacation. Marc's eldest son and his wife told us that there was a great town where the real estate prices were still low.

We fell in love with Punta Gorda as every night we watched world-class sunsets from our room. A few nights before we were going to leave we saw a listing for a condo that looked out at a vast stretch of water.

Within an hour of seeing the place we signed a purchase and sale agreement. As we drove to the realtor's office, we applied for mortgage approval on the phone. The broker, when he heard we had different last names, asked, "Are you married?" We were thrilled to be able to apply as a married couple for a mortgage on the home of our dreams.

My husband is a hard-working mediator who works for the Commonwealth of Massachusetts. He is also the kind of man who wants to give his wife everything that he can. There are things you can do married that you cannot do as a single person – wonderful things. These are the blessings that I want you to have in your life.

Being married allowed us to create the life of our dreams together. We have this home on the water in addition to our Boston condo. We feel abundant and blessed.

Finding love in your later years is not for the faint of heart.

But it can be done and the result is worth the effort.

Looking for Love

"Looking for love in too many faces,
searching their eyes and looking for traces of
what I'm dreaming of.
Hoping to find a friend and a lover;
I'll bless the day I discover another heart looking for love"

- Sung by Johnny Lee

Have you been "unlucky in love?" You may have been through a few serious relationships, or even a few marriages, that did not last. This doesn't mean that they were bad relationships, just that they did not last for a lifetime.

What we learned about love early in our lives colors how we choose mates and how we relate to them. I'm sure you have reflected a lot on your patterns in relationships and don't want to repeat the bad ones again. A lifetime of learning is a valuable resource to draw on to choose a good and loving partner.

Before we dive into the first practice, I will share with you some of my own patterns in love. Perhaps you will see yourself in some of them. But more importantly I want you to see that you can learn to upgrade your own patterns to create the kind of love you want to have in your life now – no matter what kind of experiences you have had.

My parents, God love them both, came ill prepared to their marriage.

My mother, a smart girl whose early ambitions were thwarted, was the daughter of a single mother who had escaped an arranged marriage.

My father, on his second marriage at age twenty-eight, was the youngest of a very large immigrant family. During World War II, the Navy placed him in the ROTC program in the engineering college at Cornell University, preparing him to be a navigator on a submarine in the Pacific Ocean.

They both had the upwardly mobile ambitions of post-war America. I was born in the 1950s, a time when everything seemed possible for a newly rising middle class in America. My brother and I went to good schools in a suburb with houses that actually had white picket fences around them. On summer evenings, we played out on the street until the last rays of sunshine. In many ways it was an idyllic childhood. That idyllic life came to a crashing halt when I was eight years old.

I know now that my parents had problems that I could not understand as a child. My father worked six days a week at his business, coming home late at night. I remember trying to stay awake late enough to see him come in the door.

My mother, who had worked before marriage, was frustrated by the role of a stay-at-home mother. She attended college when we were in grade school.

Their marriage looked good on the outside, with a beautiful home that they had built together. But actually they lived parallel lives, rarely spending time together, and their marriage slowly disintegrated.

Underlying the surface were deeper issues: my father's drinking, which after their divorce turned into full blown alcoholism, and my mother's emotional instabilities, rooted in her own upbringing by a young and unhappy mother.

They fought loudly, and both confided their unhappiness to me. In my childhood anger, I could only shout back at them, "I will never get married!" They divorced when I was fourteen.

After I went away to college, I didn't feel like I had a home to return to, so, paradoxically, I married shortly after graduation. My husband also came from an unhappy family. He had watched his mother die of alcoholism over many years. His parents did not divorce, but co-existed in a painful and unhappy home.

I am telling you the shortest possible version of this story because I want you to understand that being happily married has never been automatically "in the cards" for me.

Still, I thought I could create a happy family by sheer willpower. I had two babies before I was twenty-eight, only to discover that their father and I had grown apart in ways that did not portend for a long and happy life together. We sadly divorced when I was twenty-nine years old.

It took me most of my thirties to recover from the loss of the dream of having a happy family. I remember putting a poem on my wall that said, "Sorrow comes to carve out spaces in the heart for joy." I desperately hoped that that was true.

I raised my children as a single mother from the time they were one and four. Their father shared physical custody of them. This allowed me to attend graduate school at Harvard, eventually earning a doctorate in education.

I developed a successful professional career as a leadership consultant. Their father stayed in my children's lives as a loving and present father.

Acceptance and gratitude were lessons I learned from weekly attendance at Al-Anon, the program for people who are affected by other people's alcoholism. This program taught me how to find happiness, even when life doesn't give us what we expect. I also took part in therapy and transformational education, especially the work of Werner Erhard, through Landmark Education. Landmark taught me how to use the power of giving my word to create new realities.

My career developed, and by time my daughter was in her senior year of high school, I was a consultant at Arthur D. Little, Inc. in Cambridge, MA, the first consulting firm in the world, a creation of M.I.T. scientists. I taught leadership and organizational learning to executives and managers in global corporations.

When my daughter was a senior in high school and heading to college, I began to have the space in my life for a serious relationship with a man. I had dated many men in my thirties, but no one had ever committed to me. I learned from a therapist that perhaps I was the one who didn't have the space to make a commitment!

Someone did, for the first time, propose marriage to me, after only four months of dating. I was overjoyed that at last I would have someone in my life I could count on. I remember the day after our wedding feeling the great relief that someone would be there for me.

I now believe that you need to know someone longer than four months before choosing to marry. It takes time to learn how they will act and react in a variety of life circumstances. Soon into the marriage, I learned about problems that were not evident early on, and our marriage went on a steady downhill slide until I finally had the courage to end it.

After both of my children went to college I took a position as Director of Leadership Development in an organization that did international development and started to travel around the globe.

The story of my Egyptian husband is a long and culturally interesting tale that I'm only going to tell the highlights of here. He was a surgeon in the ministry of health and he supported my project to bring transformational leadership development to the front-line of health care workers in poor countries.

With the U.S. Agency for International Development's support, we built a *Leadership Development Program* that eventually went to forty-five developing nations. We personally taught the program in Afghanistan, Kenya, Tanzania, Uganda, and other countries in Africa and the Middle East. It was an experience that changed my life in many ways. I documented some of the stories from that period in my book *Leading for Results*.

I was not planning on marrying again. After two attempts, I was sure this was not something that I was good at. But I was working and living in cultures that did not allow intimate relationships outside of marriage. In order to travel and work closely together, we needed to be married. At first I only agreed to a wedding in Egypt. But when we decided to live in America, I reluctantly agreed to an American marriage. That relationship began to deteriorate soon after the wedding.

As embarrassing as it is to say I've been divorced three times, I know that I haven't done anything wrong. I married with good intentions, and ended the marriages when I found they were bringing me to emotional places I could not withstand.

After the initial heartbreak of the ending of my first marriage with my children's father, I recovered and I remain on very good terms with him to this day. We have three grandchildren together and spend Christmas, Thanksgiving, and children's birthdays together at my daughter's house. Everything that I have learned to clear my head and heart of the disappointments of failed expectations has served me to have a peaceful relationship with my children's father.

To bring the story full circle, through lots of self-development work I have also cleared the disappointments of my early family life. I know that my parents did the very best that they could. They loved me and they were committed to my having a great life. I'm deeply appreciative of all that they gave me, despite their own challenges. I have only love in my heart for both of them.

The Critical Success Factors for Finding Love

You need to resolve all relationship patterns from the past that no longer work for you. This means getting past holding regrets or resentments in your heart or mind. This completion with my parents, as well as the completions with former husbands, gives me the ability today to be in a loving marriage today.

Through this work I was able, finally, to choose a loving husband, someone who would take care of me – something I had always desired, but wasn't able to make happen. I'm glad I lived long enough, and learned enough, to have this in my life.

I've shared my story with you in the hope that you can see that, even in the face of many setbacks, it is possible to have love in your life. The key is to be willing to learn more about the most important of all human endeavors – how to love and be loved. In the next chapters I will tell you exactly what I did, so that you too can live "happily *even* after."

The Five Practices for Finding Love

"You can get it if you really want.
But you must try, try and try, try and try.
You'll succeed at last."
- Sung by Jimmy Cliff

Finding love later in life is not an easy thing to do. There are some core practices that you need to learn and engage in if you want to be successful. I will outline the five practices in this chapter. Each practice will be explained in detail in later chapters, which also include reflection questions and exercises that you can do. These practices emerged from my lifelong research about the practices that empower people to have the results they most want in life. I have combined this work with my more recent research on finding happy, healthy love to arrive at a set of practices to get results in the area of relationships. I coach women to use these practices to bring love into their lives.

Below is an in-depth overview of each one.

Practice One: Clarify Your Intention

Intentionality is the critical practice to launch any endeavor in life. You need to be clear about what you are intending to create, and you need to return to your intention when you face setbacks.

Oftentimes when I tell single women that they can find a husband in their later years, they are intrigued at first, and then quickly their conversations turn to the many disappointments they have faced in their lives in the area of love, and how they have given up. A woman in her sixties told me that the only kind of dates she now has are "fruits in a box." (It took me a minute to fully visualize dates as fruits.)

If having a partner is important to you, don't be ambivalent about it.

By setting a clear intention, and telling this intention to a committed listener, you will be able to break through a seemingly impenetrable wall. Practice One will show you how set an intention powerful enough to sustain yourself on the path to getting the love you deserve.

Practice Two: Envision Love Now

When I use the word "envision," I don't just mean just visualizing a future. I want you to use all of your senses to create, in the present moment, the experience of love that you are intending to create. We know that what we imagine can actually shape the realities we bring into our lives. Our minds act as movie projectors, projecting our beliefs out into the world.

If you want to have love in your life, you begin by living a life of love, in your thoughts, in your heart, and in your relationships with others. You will learn how to *be* the experience that you want to have.

I learned from Katherine Woodward Thomas's *Calling in "The One"* that an important place to do this is in the home. Set up your home up as a place that is ready for a partner. In my case, this meant buying a sofa that was big enough for two to stretch out on and having a bedroom with two comfortable lounge chairs and two bedside tables.

When my husband came into my home when we were first dating, he was struck by how warm and welcoming it was. Women create homes in our hearts, our bodies, and our houses. Men are drawn to the warmth this creates. I jokingly say that women should put photos of their sofas on their online dating profile pages.

In the chapter on Practice Two you will learn more about how to be ready with a loving heart and home when the right man appears.

Practice Three: Learn How to Date Online

Welcome to the Brave New World of online dating. Odds are that this is where your soulmate is!

The good news is that you don't actually date online; you only go online to get access to a "catalogue" of eligible men. Then you have to meet them in person to see if this is someone you would like to date. Don't waste time forming online "relationships." You actually need to meet people in person. I will share tips on how to do this well.

Setting up a profile that describes who you are, getting the right photos, learning how to reach out and respond to men online – these are new skills for most of us. There are lots of sites that give good advice on how to do this.

Practice Three will tell you how to be successful at online dating.

Practice Four: Learning How to Deal with the Disappointments of Dating

Dating is not for the faint of heart! The experience can be fraught with setbacks. In fact, the very nature of dating is that it is filled with disappointments. It makes sense that the majority of people you meet will not be a match for you. This is why you will need to return to your intention over and over again. This is why support is critical in this process. Every disappointment can throw you back into a sense of despair. You will need wise guidance to get through it.

I met forty men over a period of two years before my husband (miraculously) appeared. During this time my heart was tugged in quite a few directions whenever prospects who at first seemed promising didn't pan out. This can go one of two ways: after an initial sense of possibility either you lose interest, or he loses interest. Both experiences can be disappointing. Whichever way it goes, in the face of setbacks it helps to have support to return to dating again.

Your heart is involved, and the heart can be a "lonely hunter." There are things you need to do to do soothe yourself when life is disappointing (as it often is in dating). Practice Four will show you how to do this.

Practice Five: Be Open to Having a (Real) Man in Your Life

Marc and I did not meet until nine months after we first saw each other's profiles. We both doubted, from the screen shots that we saw of each other, whether we were a match for each other. I thought he was too much of a "hippie." He thought that I was too "corporate." It was only after I felt I had gone through every other nearby eligible man that I reached out to him. (It turns out that we are both somewhat in the middle on the spectrum between "corporate" and "hippie.")

Getting together was challenging. I am a phone person. In fact much of my coaching work is based on forming relationships on the phone. My husband, on the other hand, is a mediator who uses the phone to schedule his work, and he is usually short and to the point on phone calls.

On our first call, he skipped any small talk to set up a time and place to meet. (He had learned over years of online dating that he needed to meet people in person to get to know them.)

His brevity took me aback. Nevertheless, I put on my "dating clothes" and prepared to go to Starbucks, planning to tell him that while he was probably a very nice man, we weren't a match.

What a surprise to learn, after an hour and a half of rich conversation, that sitting there was a wonderful man… who would be my future husband.

Practice Five will show you how to give up your assumptions and preconceptions and become open to having real men show up.

Practice One –

Clarify your Intentions

*The first thing that happens when any of us have the
courage to set an intention, is that life begins to realign
itself around the realization of that intention.
This will sometimes occur as breakdowns and chaos.*

*In fact, Joseph Campbell once said, "Destruction is
the first act of creation."*

*Life will suddenly look as though it is not working.
Breakups, losses, disappointments, endings
and breakdowns are all the first stage of life's
rearrangement.*
– Katherine Woodward Thomas

Intention is the key to accomplishing anything great in life. Merriam Webster defines intention as "determination to act in a certain way." It has its origin in the Latin, "intendere": to turn one's attention, literally "to stretch out." Intentions are efforts that require our attention and our "stretching" to achieve them.

An interesting secondary definition of intention is "purpose with respect to marriage," as in, "*What are your intentions, young man?*" So, clarifying your intentions is particularly apropos as we begin the work of finding a husband. You will set your own intention for a committed relationship.

I find that it is useful to have intentions in all kinds of relationships. For example, with my daughter, a beautiful grown woman with three children of her own, my intention is to be a close and loving presence, someone she can confide in and trust. I work all of the time at that intention, and our relationship is ever-expanding.

My son is an incredible man who has taken on many challenges in his work and personal life. With him, my intention is to be there to listen to him and support him through all his challenges. I let him know this intention, and he expresses his appreciation for my support. In both of these relationships, my intention serves as a homing device that keeps me on course to being in a loving relationship.

If you want to be in a relationship with a man, you need to clarify exactly what you want. Don't be ambivalent about wanting a loving and committed partner. And if you want to make your intention really powerful, put a date on it. By what day, month, year do you want to realize your intention? As you move toward that date, you will strive to close the distance between your intention and the result you achieve.

When I was intending to find my true love, I first set an intention to call him in by my fifty-ninth birthday. Well, you know what happened? The right one didn't show up by my fifty-ninth birthday. A nice man did show up for a brief relationship that year, but he wasn't someone I chose to commit to.

Fortunately, I had learned what you do when you don't realize an intention. You reset it and recommit to it! So I reset my intention to call in a committed partner by my sixtieth birthday. And, boy, did this intention focus me, especially in the months before my birthday when he still hadn't shown up.

If you are like me, someone who likes to accomplish things in life, setting an intention creates a deadline that you will work hard to meet. We know for a fact that productivity increases as one gets closer to a deadline.

My sixtieth birthday was coming up in April. In December, I went out with a promising man for three dates, until a moment came when we knew that the chemistry wasn't there for either of us. What a disappointment.

Because I had set my intention, in January I went right back online and started to date another nice man. After the third date, he sent me a note telling me he was seeing two women at once, and had decided to commit to being in a relationship with the other woman.

I sent a polite note back, saying, "Ouch, and I wish you all the best" which I did. There is prayer that says, "Thank you, God, for everything you've given me, and everything you took away." I accepted this as not meant to be, and went back online – again.

I had been online for almost two years at this point. I wasn't sure if there were any other likely candidates in the Boston area on Match.com that I hadn't reached out to. But my intention to call in a committed partner by my sixtieth birthday kept me going.

I had seen Marc's profile nine months previous to this, and had sent a brief note and hadn't heard back from him. But time was ticking, so I sent another note and was surprised to hear back from him this time.

As I described in the last chapter, after our initial phone call I was convinced that I was going to go down to Starbucks (fortunately the one in my neighborhood) to meet a man and tell him that we weren't a match.

What an incredible pleasure to find a sweet, kind, interesting (and handsome!) man, the father of five grown children, an attorney who became a mediator who works with parents of special needs children and schools.

We spent over an hour talking. I learned that he had served in Vietnam. He learned that I had traveled to Afghanistan to train health managers and their teams in the midst of the war there. We appreciated each other's adventurous outlook towards life.

I was so glad when he sent a note the next day telling me how much he had liked meeting me and that he wanted to see me again.

We had gone on only four dates when I started to plan my sixtieth birthday party. As part of my coaching work I had been taking on a new statement of my identity: "I am deeply connected with others and others are connected with me." This replaced an old false childhood belief that I was alone in the world. The new adult belief gave me the courage to invite everyone I loved to my party.

Lifelong friends from every decade of my life were invited. I even invited my children's father! This was the gathering of family and friends that I invited Marc to after our fourth date. His response was, "Are you sure you want me to come?" I replied, "Why not?" I knew he was a kind and caring man.

He came to the party looking very nice in a tweed jacket. I wasn't able to spend exclusive, or hardly any, time with him, but he did well with my friends and family. In fact, one couple that he spent time with that night later became close friends of ours.

After I went around the room introducing everyone, from my childhood through my more recent friends from my fifties, I finally turned to Marc, and said, "And then there's Marc," and smiled. I had no idea what would happen with this relationship or what it would mean in my sixties. I only knew that I was standing inside of an intention to have a good man in my life.

Marc and I dated for three months. And I mean dated, as in he called me up to arrange a date, picked me up, we went out and did something fun, and then he drove me home and kissed me goodbye at the door.

When people asked him why he dated like this, he said he wanted to get to know me as a friend first, before sleeping with me. And we became great friends. We started by bicycling together and that expanded into a life in which we are friends, family, and lovers.

This all came about because I set a clear intention – to have a loving and committed man in my life by my sixtieth birthday.

Marc far exceeded my expectations. He is devoted to me, and would do anything for my happiness. I have never known a man like him before. He really is a throwback to another generation, in all the right ways. He is "old fashioned" when it comes to marriage. He believes in family and fidelity. He ended his first marriage several decades after the relationship had dissolved. He stayed to raise his children, as good men often do.

Once he realized that he was in love with me, he was committed to me and to our relationship and proposed to me many times. I waited for two years to see him in a variety of settings before accepting.

Set Your Intention

Your intention will help you to face many challenges and overcome many obstacles. You will need to communicate this intention with at least one other person who will hold you to your commitment.

It is important to state your intention in the positive. A common error people make when writing intentions is that they write down what they don't want rather than focusing on what they do want. Say, "I want a committed man," rather than "I want to stay away from people who are commitment-phobic."

You can write your intention as if it is happening now. For example, I wrote, "My true love is successfully completing issues in his life so that he will be free to create a shared life together." That was my intention for many months as I was waiting for my beloved to show up. And in fact this turned out to be true – I met Marc just four weeks after one of his sons completed many years recovering from addictions. His son continues to do well today.

Don't write an intention that states you are "trying" to do something. You don't want to be in process of "trying" to get what you want. Saying "I will try to date two new men this month" has a very different energy than "I *will* date two new men this month."

Be aware that old "false beliefs" from earlier periods of your life can color your intentions. For example "I am unlovable" or "I am too needy" may be beliefs that come from experiences you had when you were young. Don't let these limit what you are intending to have now in your life.

The great thing about getting older is that you begin to know your own value. Even if you have had a poor history of relationships, it is never too late to learn how to love and be loved. People grow and change. Be sure that your intentions reflect how you value yourself in the present.

Remember:
- *Write your intention in a way that comes from your current mature valuing of yourself*
- *Communicate your intention with a committed listener*
- *Be careful what you ask for; you just might get it!*

Writing Your Intention

An intention statement is a concise statement that captures, in as few words as possible, what you commit to having in a relationship. For example, "I intend to be in a loving committed relationship by the end of this year."

Exercise to Discover Your Intention

Ask yourself:

- *Am I willing to commit to having an intimate relationship in my life?*
- *By when will I intend for this love to come into my life?*
- *Who can be my "committed listener" to hold this intention with me?*

Writing the Intention Statement

Fill in the blanks in this sentence:

I intend to _____ by _____.

For example:

I intend to be in a committed monogamous relationship by December of this year.

Or

I intend to be married by my sixty-second birthday.

Write a draft of an Intention Statement and read it aloud.

- Ask yourself: Does it ring true?
- When you hear it, do you say "Yes!"?

I have found that when people say "Yes!" to an Intention Statement, that statement is usually right. When they hesitate or say "Yeah," they need to do a little more work to find the exact intention that resonate in their hearts.

Your Intention Statement is like a ship's rudder that will steer you through this next passage in your life. Once you have clarified your intention you can go on to the other practices for finding the committed man of your dreams.

Who will you share your intention with today?

Practice Two –

Envision Love Fulfilled

*"I had a vision of love and it was
all that you turned out to be."*
– Sung by Mariah Carey

ariah Carey sings passionately about her vision of love, believing in it and waiting patiently for her dream to be realized. This may seem overly romantic to you, but this is actually what you need to do to manifest great love in your life. You need to reignite your ability to dream. As George Lucas, creator of *Star Wars* said, "Dreams are extremely important. You can't do it unless you can imagine it."

Right before I met Marc I framed a picture of John Lithgow, the actor known for his role in *3rd Rock from the Sun* and looked at it every day. I wanted someone that sweet, that loving, and especially that big! I kept that image in my mind's eye as I prepared for a wonderful man to enter my life.

Like all of us, you have had disappointments in your life. But those disappointments don't negate your human ability, and right, to dream of a better future. Forming a picture of a desired future is the heart of imagination, that uniquely human capability that we all have. It is a precious gift that we need to nurture and use well.

I have found that all of my clients, even Afghan health workers in the midst of war, are capable of dreaming of a better future. These health workers imagined "*Healthy children walking to schools on safe roads,*" and went to work increasing health services for children to bring that vision into reality. They used their human capability to imagine a better future. You can too!

A vision helps you to see what you want to bring into existence. The images that you hold in your mind shape your choices and actions. Use the wonderful human capability to imagine to envision your future with love fulfilled.

Many years ago, while riding on a ferry, I watched a man sitting with his family. He had a big smile on his face as he put his arms around all of them, holding them close in a loving way. I'll never forget that picture in my mind. This was my vision of love. At our first meeting Marc gave me a warm and loving hug that boded well for our future! He *always* wants to hold me and love me. He fulfills my long-held dream of what love could look and feel like.

How Does Envisioning Work?

We continuously create images in our daily lives that guide our actions. For example, when we wake up in the morning, we see in our mind visual images of what we plan to do next – eating breakfast or traveling to work. These images guide us out of bed and into action.

Once you see an image of yourself doing something you intend to do, you start to act in ways that will move you closer to it. This is the way your brain moves you from image to action in everyday life. We try things on in our minds before we act on them. Our thoughts are "trial actions." The images in our brain create pathways that we move towards. You can use this human capability to bring love into your life.

Reflection – Ask Yourself:

- *What aspects of love do you want to bring into your life?*
- *What images of love fulfilled inspire you?*
- *What do you imagine it will feel like to be with your beloved?*

Katherine Woodward Thomas taught me how take my clients through a *Vision Meditation* to visualize using all of the senses. I've included some of the questions from this meditation below.

Exercise: Vision Meditation

In preparation:

- Imagine being grateful that your beloved is already in your life. Don't attach to this to a specific person. You don't know who is coming yet!
- Allow yourself to drop into the feelings that are present between you and your beloved.

Meditate on the following questions:

- What does it look like, sound like, smell like, to have your beloved in your life?
- What does it feel like to have your beloved be responsive to your needs?
- What's your ideal day with your beloved (speak it as though it is happening in present time)?

I take my clients through this guided meditation to create visions they can live into. Below is the vision I created when I went through this meditation prior to meeting my husband Marc:

I am deeply grateful that I am with a partner for life who can meet me at the deepest level-
A match for me who is physically, emotionally, spiritually and financially healthy.
He is an intimate friend who is emotionally present- with great depth and relational intelligence.
He is fit and I love to put my arms around him-I feel comforted in his embrace.
We have a strong sexual sensuous loving connection.
He is a true spiritual partner- who is interested in evolution and growth.
And he has a matching intellectual curiosity and sense of humor!
He appreciates me the way I am and is based in Boston.
We are at a point in our lives where we enjoy our work and have time to enjoy life outside of work.
He shares my pride and joy in our children and grandchildren.
As I prepare for his impending arrival, I am relaxed, trusting and thankful to God.
Thank you for bringing this gift of love into my heart and my life.

I wrote my Vision of Love Fulfilled in 2013. This vision created a resonance that I lived inside of until Marc arrived in early 2014. He fits this description to a "T"!

Try this meditation yourself. Speak your answers to the questions out loud. Capture the words and write them down as you are talking. Then keep this vision near your bedside and read it often!

Living in the Field of Your Vision

A vision creates a field of possibilities. You start to see something that previously was not there for you. For example, when you decide to buy a certain model of car, all of a sudden you see that car everywhere.

To prepare to manifest love in your life begin to "act as if" it is true. Then you will *be* in love.

How do you do this?

To be in love, prior to your beloved appearing, cultivate love and loving in your life. Don't wait for someone else to bring you love. Create it in every way that you can.

In the years prior to Marc arriving, I started to take vacations with extended family. We spent love-filled time together. For my sixtieth birthday, I invited all of the people I love to my home. Marc came into the field of love that was already in my life. Be sure to spend loving time with the people you already love.

Create a Clearing for Love to Enter Your Life

I set up my life and my physical world to receive love. I made sure that there was time in my schedule for relaxation and being with people I enjoyed. I set up my home to be a welcoming space for a beloved to join me. I put two large armchairs in my bedroom where we could have long talks. I bought a big sofa that two could spread out on. My dining table was ready for a couple to sit down to eat together.

When Marc first came into my home, he was struck by the feeling of warmth and space for him. I could tell that he wanted to stay!

My clients have been very creative in how they welcome a man into their homes. Some put an extra bedside table and lamp by their bed. ("The bedside table technique worked well," one client wrote me after a sweet man fell in love with her.) Another client made sure to have fresh flowers in her home so that beauty is always present. All of these actions build the field of love in your life. And into that field a good man will feel welcomed.

Reflection Questions:

- How are you bringing more love into your life now?
- What changes have you made in your home?
- What changes have you made in your schedule?

When she was single, Katherine wrote an aspirational love song about her intended reading her David Whyte poems by the fire. And wouldn't you know, when her beau was courting her he sent her a David Whyte poem. How transcendent – beyond the realm of every day experience – is that! Use your artistic abilities to express your dreams of love.

You can be as creative as you want with your vision. I like to use words, but have found that images impact the brain in a special way. Over the years I have created many *Vision Boards* and encourage all of my clients to create them. Miraculously, everything that I put on these boards eventually manifests in my life. I have pasted pictures of homes, handsome men, engagement rings, healthy older women exercising, and even babies (for my daughter, not me!). And all of these things came into my life.

I cannot recommend a *Vision Board* highly enough. The instructions to do this are below.

Exercise: Vision of Love Fulfilled
Creating a Vision Board

You will need:
- A pile of magazines that you can cut up – with good pictures in them (usually ads)
- A large piece of poster board that is firm enough to hold pictures pasted on it
- A pair of scissors and a glue stick
    1. Pick up a magazine and tear out any images that call to you about love. *Don't do a lot of thinking about this. Choose whatever images call to you; later you can reflect on what in the images spoke to you, and which images you want to keep in your vision.*

        You might be surprised by what attracts you. Let romantic love images co-exist with images of other passions in your life, including home, family, friends, causes, etc.
    2. Trim the images with scissors or leave them with torn edges if you prefer them that way.
    3. Arrange them on the poster board, moving them around until the pattern pleases you, and then attach the pictures to the board using a glue stick.
    4. Once you have assembled the images, study the overall collage. Which aspects of it are calling to you most strongly? What do you see about how *Love Fulfilled* looks?

5. Place your vision board where you will see it regularly – near your breakfast table, on your mirror, or beside your desk – and look at it every day. This is the future you are creating.

Enjoy your vision of love. This is the field that your true love will enter.

The next chapter will tell you more of the nuts and bolts of how to date. We need to have dreams, but we also need to put foundations under them. As the saying goes, "*Dream big, start small, act now!*"

Learn how to Navigate the World of Online Dating

"Before you take a man and say I do, now,
make sure he's in love with you.
My mama told me, you better shop around...
Good looking guys come a dime a dozen.
Try to find you one who's gonna give you true lovin'"
– Sung by Captain and Tennille

M y client, Lisa, was excited to meet a new man. They had talked on the phone and had a good conversation. When they met he was kind and interesting. She checked in with her feelings, and found herself to be comfortable and attracted. But when two days went by with no word from him Lisa sank into despair. She didn't know what to make of his behavior. She sent me this note:

Dear Joan:

I met Karl last Friday. It was a lovely dinner, I felt very comfortable with him.

Saturday he traveled to another city and he did not contact me that day. Sunday in the morning I sent a link about a movie we had been talking about. He answered me late at night, "I really liked your company, but I felt that you had no interest in me."

His message surprised me a lot, I answered that I enjoyed his company too and if he could explain what I did to make him think that I had not liked him.

He wrote to me early this morning that he was sleepy and later he wrote telling me that today he has a long day traveling.

These messages created a lot of anxiety in me. I am working to recognize my feelings and my thoughts and to calm myself down. Thanks for helping me to move forward wisely.

I responded,

Lisa, this is the uncertainty of online dating. By its nature, dating leads to disappointment and anxiety, because you don't know this person and you don't know how they are going to act.

I remember the first online date I went on. He was a very nice man, and I was very surprised when he didn't follow up. So I sent him a message. He was honest and said he was not that interested in me. It was a shock to me as we had had a nice conversation.

There is a male dating coach, Evan Marc Katz. Reading his posts online will help you to understand how men respond when dating, and what they won't tell you.

I highly recommend reading this to maintain your sanity while you meet many new men on the path to finding the one who will be crazy about you!

Sending love, Joan

Welcome to the brave new world of online dating: a world with unclear rules and expectations. A world you will have to learn to navigate. But no matter how daunting this world may seem to you, odds are that this is where your soulmate is.

How can the generation who came late to the technology and social media party keep up with the mores and practices of this new world?

You will need to learn to face the many challenges of online dating, including:

- How do you create a profile that represents you well?
- What photos should you post?
- How do you reach out to men you don't know?
- What to do if you don't get responses?
- How do you safely meet strangers?
- How do you sustain yourself in the face of rejections?

And how do you get confidence presenting yourself when you don't look like you did in your younger days? What do you do about these extra lines on your face, or extra pounds on your hips?

You may be plagued with questions including:

- *Will a man ever want me?*
- *Don't men only want younger women?*
- *Don't men only want sex?*

You would love to have the companionship of a compatible man, but do you have to meet so many "losers" or be "rejected" by so many potential partners to find him?

If you're not sure you can do this, you're not alone. Women who are dating online are finding that they need a lot of help and support to get through this maze. And help is available. There is an entire industry built around providing advice for online dating. There are sites and coaches and newsletters.

Start doing your research. If you needed to find a job, you would learn how to navigate the world of online job searching. And you would be persistent in the face of failure or rejection. You need to apply the same kind of commitment to your love life.

It's just as important.

"Keep Fishing": Sue's Story

Sue shared with me what it was like to be divorced at age sixty after a thirty-eight-year marriage to someone she had met in high school. She told me, *"I didn't know how to date!"*

Through activities like singles groups she met a few people. And she went online for a year, but it was hard:

- *People she liked didn't respond to her.*
- *People who responded to her weren't great matches.*

One guy who she went out with for a few dates wrote her to say they weren't compatible. *"That hurt!"*

But she was determined. *"I really did want someone in my life to grow old with."*

With coaching she learned how to set up a good profile and how to reach out to men online. She learned that for every five people she wrote to, maybe one would respond. She learned:

- *It doesn't mean anything if a man doesn't respond*
- *Don't take every "rejection" personally*
- *Meet many new people and stay open-minded*

She went on "coffee dates" to meet a variety of new men, and met almost thirty people over a two-year period. It wasn't easy, she says, *"I wanted to quit at certain moments."*

The coaching encouraged her to keep going: *"You're doing well, you've caught a few (that you tossed back). Keep fishing!"* Shortly afterwards Sue met someone who shares not only her values, but a common set of friends from their youth. They are now into their fifth year of happily loving each other.

You have a lot of love and energy you want to give someone. If you want a partner to share this precious time of life, *"Don't give up! Keep fishing!"*

How to Online Date

First of all, there is no such thing as "online dating." Remember, you don't date online - you date in person. You only go online to get access to available men. I discovered that there were thousands of sixty-year-old men in the Boston area who were single and wanted a relationship. I only learned this by going on Match.com. These men were not approaching me in the grocery store, they were not at my worksite, and my friends did not know any good single available men.

It was the encouragement of my thirty-year-old son that got me started online. I learned quickly that you don't really know much about men from their profiles. People can say anything online. You need to meet them in person to learn anything real about them. I got to the point that if someone was in the right age group, looked reasonable, lived near me, and appeared to be educated, I would contact him.

Pick dating sites that seem interesting to you. I have clients who have found their true love on *Our Time, Senior Singles, Elite Singles, Match.com* and *Spiritual Singles*. No site is magic. They are just locations where people (like you) are looking for available people to date. Try one or two. Put up a profile and some good photos and see what happens. If no one reaches out to you, reach out to a few people. Put your foot in the water!

Be Cautious When Meeting New People in Person

You can assume that the majority of people on these sites are well meaning and want to find someone to date. But they may be looking for different things – anywhere from a one-night stand to marriage. It is good to write on your profile that you are looking for a long-term committed relationship. I found that most men in their sixties are looking for relationships.

Look at Lots of Profiles to See If There Is Something You Have in Common

If you think there is some commonality, it is ok to send them a brief note and see if they respond. If you are not getting responses, have someone look at your profile and give you feedback. It's all right to say things that you believe may be "deal breakers" for someone. Better to let them know those things upfront.

For example, I have a client who is six feet tall, has a PhD in biochemistry, and is from Germany. These might be intimidating factors for some men. She posted these on the front page of her profile. Who did she find online and end up marrying? A six-foot-four professor of European history who continues to be fascinated with her many years later.

Men are visual. Make sure you have good (current) photos of yourself. Don't include pictures of anyone else, not kids or friends – just you. Only include recent photos. You want to be easily recognized when you first meet someone. Show that you are happy!

But don't be dismayed when the majority of them don't respond back. It doesn't mean anything about you.

You can exchange a few messages with a man, and then arrange to call him. But you don't want to accumulate online chat buddies, or phone buddies. After a one or two messages on the site and one or two calls to see if you like him, arrange to meet.

Block Your Phone Number When You Call Him

This is a stranger that you might not want having your number. Before I learned this, I gave my number to a man who got irate when, after our call, I decided I did not want to meet him. He called back several times. This made me nervous. After that I called the men, and blocked my number so they couldn't see it. (A simple procedure where I live; you press *6 before dialing.) Some women get a dedicated phone number just for online dating.

After speaking with a man, if you both have some interest, you meet them for coffee in a safe public place.

Don't give men your address before you know them. Drive yourself to meet them. Don't have anyone pick you up, and don't go to anyone's house on the first date.

You have a right at any time, during messaging, after talking on the phone, or after meeting them for coffee, to send them a polite note that says, "You seem like a nice man, but I don't think we are a match." Do this in writing. You don't want to get into a discussion about your feelings with a man you don't know.

You probably will need to meet lots of men in person. I met forty men over two years. That's not so bad – meeting two men a month for coffee is not that difficult. What *is* difficult is weathering the emotional ups and downs of dating. You get your hopes up only to have them dashed - when either he does not live up to your expectations, or you do not live up to his.

Learn How to Meet Men Who Aren't Right for You Without Giving Up!

Most good men who are not superficial are looking for someone in their own age group. I asked my husband why he was interested in someone his own age and this is what he told me: his son was forty years old and he did not want to be in relationship with someone in his son's generation. He also did not want to date someone who was in a different stage of life, i.e., still in active childrearing.

Marc had raised five children and was ready to move on to the next phase of his life. One of our first conversations was, "Do you have kids in the house?" When we learned that neither of us did, it was a signal to us both to proceed.

We have a wonderful life together that includes talking with and seeing our grown children and grandchildren. But day-to-day we have the glorious freedom of a life without children in the house.

Appearances Count, but Not as Much as You Think

The Dutch have a saying, "There is a lid for every pot." This is exceptionally good news for all of us who are not fashion models. I learned that many men were attracted to me – and that there were an equal number who were not. There is no accounting for taste. You cannot know why a man is attracted to a woman. But unless he is, not much is going to happen.

Appearance matters. I won't lie. But not in the way you might think. I am, and have been for many years, at least thirty pounds overweight. I dress well and care about my appearance. I try to look as good as possible. I wear makeup when I have to, but don't particularly like it.

I put makeup on for the photos I took for my profile, and I would wear makeup when I went to meet men, so that I looked like the photos in my profile. Only later did I learn that those professional photos intimidated my husband when he saw them. He thought I looked too "corporate!"

I think I am an average looking woman. (My husband thinks I'm beautiful, so that's good enough for me!) I have a good heart and I am very curious and adventurous about life, and I think those qualities came through to good men. Over the course of two years, many men wanted to see me for a second or third date, and some of them wanted to pursue a relationship.

I learned, from coaching, how to check in with myself about how I was feeling when I was meeting new men. I would "ground myself" in my seat and put my attention on my feelings. I did this rather than putting attention on whether he liked me, or even on assessing whether he had all the characteristics I wanted in a man.

My most important monitor was how I was feeling when I was with him. This turned out to be a great way to judge the likelihood of this being a man I would be comfortable with.

In the two years of "dating" (mostly "meeting") men, I pursued only one relationship that lasted three months. You can learn a lot in three months, enough to know if this is someone you want to invest more time in. There were several men that I had two or three dates with, only to learn that one (or both) of us did not have enough interest to pursue a relationship.

Give the Men a Break

Men don't know how to do online dating either, you know.

I wasn't drawn to Marc's profile at first because I thought he might be too much of a hippie. It turns out we are both children of the sixties and seventies and have a great deal in common, including music, culture, and attitudes toward life and raising children.

But he didn't talk much on the phone when I called to set up our meeting, so, being a great talker myself, I assumed we would have nothing in common. I went to my first date with Marc, planning to tell him, "You seem like a nice man, but we're not a match..." only to discover that I was drawn to his kindness and his manliness.

One hiccup was that when he ordered his cup of coffee he paid for his own and didn't offer to pay for mine. I just looked at him and paid for my own coffee. Now, you have to understand; my husband is a generous man who would gladly pay for a stranger's coffee in Starbucks. But he had recently been told by a woman he had dated that it was insulting for him to pay for a woman's food. So he was trying to learn the "new rules" of dating.

I decided to overlook this, and it's a good thing I did. From that day to this, Marc has paid for every single meal out together. This fits with his early upbringing that taught him to care for women.

Marc sent me a note the day after our first date, saying he was interested in seeing me again. I was elated. I had learned that if a man is genuinely interested he won't waste time before letting you know. (I learned that from my son!)

But even then our relationship started slowly. I went on a trip right after we met, and then he was sick the following week and I didn't hear from him. Two weeks after we met, when I still hadn't seen him, I sent him a brief text saying hello. I did this just to get closure on what I thought was another failed attempt.

I had learned, and strongly recommend, not to pursue men if they don't show interest. A man who is interested will get in touch with you. Pursuing them will not make you feel attractive, and will not let them feel that they are courting you. So I was following my own advice, and sent a text only to be sure that this was really over.

To my surprise Marc texted back immediately and asked if we could meet that afternoon. We had a lovely walk around Jamaica Pond and then went to eat in a Thai restaurant. (He paid for that meal after I told him it was fine with me.) He kissed me goodbye in the parking lot. And I kissed him back.

Still, I didn't know for sure where this was going when I didn't hear from him again for another week. When the following Friday came around I was sure it was over again. I remember telling my hairdresser on Friday at 5 p.m. that this relationship was a non-starter. He called me at 6 p.m. to ask to see me that weekend.

Marc! (He now apologizes endlessly for those unsettling weeks.)

At this point, on the third date, I let him pick me up at my home. I showed him my condo and he liked the warmth of it. We had a lovely long date, with a walk through a college campus, and then a movie that I picked out. And then he dropped me off at my house, kissed me goodbye, and I didn't hear from him for another week. Oy vey.

After three months of this, I got the courage to ask him if he would ever be interested in going away for a weekend. The way his smile lit up his face reassured me that this was not going to be a platonic friendship.

I planned a romantic getaway by the sea. We were so comfortable by this time that getting into bed felt completely natural and relaxed. We had already been through a lot, including his meeting all my friends and relatives at my birthday party.

Since then I have asked Marc many times why he wanted to wait so long before sleeping with me. He said he wanted to be sure we could be friends first. *Now that's a man worth waiting for.*

The day after our weekend away he texted me, "Oh no, I think I'm in love with you!" I wondered, was this a problem? Texting is not my favored means of communicating, especially communicating emotions. But he later explained that he was shocked because he thought he was never going to fall in love again.

From a man who could be out of touch for a week at a time, Marc transformed into someone who always wanted to be with me. It was remarkable how different it was after he fell in love with me. Today, five years later, he still always wants to be by my side. But to get there, I had to pass through dating. You cannot expect men to act like they are in a relationship with you when they are first getting to know you. This means that their communication may not be as regular as you wish it to be in a relationship.

Early stages of dating are not easy. But you have to go through them to meet your sweetheart.

Is Online Dating Right for You?

Anne, age sixty-six, didn't think she would find a man online who would be her match. "I'm kind of different. I'm more Birkenstock and veggies than heels and martinis."

But when a friend posted her profile on "Spiritual Singles," a lovely man who was vegan (as she is) and into jazz music responded.

She found someone who shares her lifestyle, including meditation, exercise, music, and travel. He is crazy about her and they recently became engaged. Their engagement is the culmination of four years of enjoying getting to know each other.

She and I talked about how great love is in this stage of life, when we are not dependent on others to "complete us." We know what is important to us, and how to enjoy life. We are looking for a partner to enjoy life with.

Dating is not for the faint of heart. Learn as much as possible about how to choose a man who will be good for you. I liked reading dating coach Evan Mark Katz posts to get a man's view of dating. I highly recommend Katherine Woodward Thomas's book, and courses on *Calling in "The One"* to more deeply understand the roots of your relationship patterns, *and how to transform them!*

If you have an intention to bring a great man into your life, and you have created a *Vision of Love Fulfilled* that inspires you, then there is some work that you have to do. Everyone wishes they could just meet the man of their dreams right off. But the truth is that you have to kiss a few frogs, or at least meet them.

The better you get at online dating, the more likely it will be for you to meet a man who shares your values – someone that you want to share your bed and your life with.

You might need help to get you back up on your feet every time someone says you're not "the one" for him and you experience "rejection." It may not be easy. Some women find their match after only a few dates. I didn't have that experience. Perhaps that was because I wasn't quite ready.

Online Dating "Do's and Don'ts"

Do: Choose an online dating service that appeals to you.
(27% of Match.com users are in the 43-72 age group. And there are thousands of them!)

Don't: Use free services; you get what you pay for.

Do: Post several good photos that clearly show a close-up your face (smiling) and you in action in a full body shot (dancing, hiking). You don't want to surprise him on meeting!

Don't: Use photos that are more than a few years old that don't look like you do now.

Do: Write a profile that communicates your interests, passions, and intentions. For good examples see: *7 Ways to Become the Type of Woman Men Fight for Online* - on Huffpost.com, and *How to Write and Unstoppable Senior Dating Profile* - on Sixtyandme.com

Do: Ask people who know you well how they would describe your strengths.

Don't: Say you like to "walk on the beach" (everyone likes that!).

Don't: Put down all the negatives that you don't want in a male companion (no one likes a complainer).

Do: Be organized and persistent – allocate at least two hours a week to reviewing the dating site and responding to people who interest you.

Don't: Randomly go online and then complain there is no one good there.

Do: Reach out to people who look interesting by sending them brief notes.

Don't: Send too many texts or email before you meet; best practice is no more than two messages and two phone calls before arranging to meet in person.

Do: Ask if you can call him -- and know how to block your number on your phone.

Don't: Give anyone you don't know (in person and well) your phone number or address!

Do: Set a clear and precise intention about what you are creating in your life, e.g. a committed partner by the end of the year.

Do: Communicate this intention to someone who will hold it for you — a good friend or a coach.

Don't: Get discouraged after the first few people you meet.

Do: Go out for coffee dates with people to meet them.

Don't: Arrange for a long dinner or activity date with anyone you don't know.

Do: Keep an open mind when meeting people.

Don't: Jump into bed before you know a man well. (No matter how much "chemistry" there is!)

Do: Give an interesting man a chance – try three dates if there is some interest there.

Don't: Assume that you are already in a relationship in the first few weeks (that is, don't expect him to text or call regularly, etc.)

Do: Know your values and your "deal breakers."

Don't: Go in with a prescribed picture of what this man looks like.

Do: Communicate kindly when choosing not to continue, i.e. via a note, "*You seem like a very nice person, but I don't think we're a match.*"

Don't: Disappear without communicating.

Do: Relax and check in with yourself to see how you are feeling on a date. Are you comfortable being with this person? Does conversation flow easily and naturally?

Don't: Conduct a job interview.

Do: Let them pursue you after the initial meeting; they know what they like.

Don't: Take it (too) personally if they decide not to continue. Its impossible to know what someone else finds attractive.

Do: Be open to meeting many people.

Don't: Get demoralized!

Do: Reach out for support.

Don't: Do this alone!

Do: Be intentional.

Don't: Give up!

Remember, the Only Way Out Is Through!

Learn to Deal with the Disappointments of Dating

"Yesterday, love was such an easy game to play
Now I need a place to hide away.
Oh, I believe in yesterday."
–The Beatles

In the months before I met Marc, I had met several men who were interesting enough to have more than one date with. I let myself be open to learning about them. One man, a financial planner, after two weeks revealed that his previous girlfriend had a restraining order out on him – not his fault, of course.

Another nice man, a PhD in Oceanography, was very interesting. But there came a moment on our third date when we both realized that there just wasn't enough chemistry for us to be a couple. A third man, a retired accountant and a widower, lived nearby, and seemed interested, but after the third date he revealed that he was dating someone else and had decided to pursue that relationship.

The very nature of dating is that it is fraught with expectations and disappointments. For every new man you meet you get your hopes up, only to find out that he does not live up to your expectations, or, that you do not live up to his. *How you deal with these disappointments is the key to your success.*

How Do You Keep Going After Multiple Disappointments?

For every disappointment we face in life, we pull up an emotional string connected to all of our past disappointments and losses. That's why we can get our heart hurt by a stranger who doesn't return a phone call.

Disappointment touches the spots in our bodies where other losses have lodged. I would find after a dating disappointment that my heart hurt so badly that I could not go on without treating it.

Honor Yourself so That Others Can Cherish You

We hear that we need to love ourselves before others can love us. But it isn't always clear how to do this. An essential part of this work is honoring your own feelings and needs. *If you don't pay attention to your feelings and needs, you won't be able to find a partner that does this for you*. This is so simple to say, and so hard to practice consistently.

In response to disappointments in early life you may have taken on false beliefs such as, "I am not lovable" or "Men can't be trusted." If so, you may be unknowingly operating from those beliefs in your life now.

You will need to upgrade these beliefs to ones that you now know to be true, such as "I am worthy of great love," and "I can trust men who prove themselves to be trustworthy." This is what is really true about the world. We don't want to be held captive by beliefs that we generated when we were children.

Your false beliefs may not be immediately visible to you. To learn more about them, look at the types of relational problems you have found yourself in. Usually these reflect some old false belief you have about yourself. For example, I have a client who frequently feels that her boyfriend is not paying enough attention to her – he is not buying her the kind of gifts she likes and is not spending the kind of time with her that she would like. She was raised by two well-meaning but overworking parents who had little time for her when she was a child. She took on early false beliefs, including, "People I love don't care about my needs."

Unfortunately she has carried this false belief into her adult relationships. When her boyfriend does not give her the kinds of gifts that she prefers, she immediately goes into feeling neglected. The false beliefs from her childhood are dictating how she experiences her love relationship today.

To break this pattern she needed to "upgrade" to a belief that is true, that she is worthy of being loved and cherished. She learned to soothe herself when she feels disappointed, rather than look to her boyfriend to do that. And the two of them are working together to upgrade the false beliefs that have origins in their early disappointments in life.

I also had false beliefs about love. After watching my parents fight for many years until they finally ended their marriage, I took on the false beliefs that "I am on my own" and "Others can't be trusted." My self-sufficient adult life was a reflection of these beliefs. It wasn't until I identified the false beliefs and saw their destructiveness in my life, that I became willing to upgrade my own beliefs about love.

With the support of my coach, Katherine, I embraced the belief that, "I am deeply connected to others and others are deeply connected to me." I began to see the truth of this statement in my adult life.

I've written in earlier chapters how this new belief had me take on new actions, including being more connected to my family and reaching out to friends more often. It also empowered me to go through the inevitable disappointments of dating without becoming disillusioned.

How Do You Transform Limiting False Beliefs?
Exercise: Adapted from *The Self-Love Power Practice* by Katherine Woodward Thomas

When you feel pain from disappointment, locate the feeling in your body. Where is the pain located – in your heart, in your gut? When you locate it, ask this part of yourself,

"What do you feel?

"What do you need?"

Then listen carefully to yourself and mirror back what you are saying, as you would if you were actively listening to a friend in need.

Say,

"I can see you're feeling hurt and neglected."

"I can see you need someone to care for you and put your needs first."

Then from your mature adult center, you reassure this hurt part of you by saying,

"Don't worry, I care about your feelings and needs. I am here for you and you can count on me!"

You do this until the hurt is relieved.

When I was dating I used this *Self-Love Power Practice* over a hundred times. It is the most played recording in my iTunes library! This practice gives you a way to love yourself when you feel let down and disappointed by others.

Upgrading Your Story about Love

Beth's Story

My client, a sixty-nine-year-old professional woman, has spent her entire adult life without a committed intimate relationship. For fifty years Beth has dated men, but no relationship lasted longer than six months. She said, "The men I like don't like me, or the men who like me I don't like."

She felt deprived of the support and care in her personal life that she so desired.

Beth is a bold and vibrant woman who still wants to live to the fullest, so she contacted me to coach her. She wanted companionship, "Someone who loves what I love to do, someone I can be adventurous with."

Though skeptical at first, she was willing to try to unravel what had gotten her into this situation over and over again.

Unpeeling the Onion

In our first conversation, Beth let me know that when she was eighteen years old her first boyfriend had broken off with her after a three-year relationship, and had started to date another woman. She had believed that this was a committed relationship, and this betrayal broke her heart.

Out of that experience she took on the belief, "I'm not lovable." She went on to create an active life, but one in which she had to be self-sufficient and take care of herself. This was a sensible course for someone who sees herself as "not lovable." From this early experience she also decided, "Men are not trustworthy."

Beth lived out the paradoxical adage, "We see what we believe." For over fifty years, she only saw men who were not reliable, or who could not be in a committed relationship.

When we first started coaching, Beth told me that she was not able to find men in her age group who were as physically, socially, and mentally as active as she was. (Beth has an MBA and had recently participated in a Triathlon.)

She had dated several men from an online site, but they were not living life fully the way that she was. She felt, "I deserve to have something more!"

I was shocked when, in our second conversation, she was very excited to report that she had met a bright witty seventy-year old widower through the same dating site she had been on. He was fit, entrepreneurial, and very interested in her. They had gone on a great date and she saw real possibility.

Just naming the false identity "I'm not lovable" allowed her to see an attractive eligible man who was interested in her.

She also took on the assignment to open up space in her life and home to bring a partner in. She already had a queen size bed, but it was set up for one person, with only one bedside table. As part of her homework she added a second bedside table. She reported, "The end table coaching worked!"

In the second month of the relationship Beth's new beau declared that he was head over heels in love with her. This surprised, delighted, and concerned her.

She was concerned that it was too early for her to commit to him. *I corroborated that this was a mature adult woman's judgment that she needed to take time getting to know him before committing.*

To break through her barriers to allowing this relationship to develop, we looked again at the decision she had made at age eighteen, that "Men can't be trusted."

As we began to explore what had happened, we saw that her teenage boyfriend had not actually left her. She had left him to go on to college, creating not only a geographic distance, but also a distance in values about what they each wanted in their lives.

So, though a tender eighteen-year-old was heartbroken at what appeared to be a betrayal, the mature woman Beth could now see that she had actually chosen to develop herself in ways that didn't include this boyfriend.

She had actually left him!

She saw that she could give up the grudge she had held against him for fifty years. More importantly she could give up the covert agreement she had made with herself, "I will never to trust a man again."

Beth now saw that she could upgrade this to a new agreement with herself, "I can trust a man who, over time, shows that he is trustworthy."

And she forgave herself for holding a grudge all those years, a grudge that had prevented her from having a rich personal life. She invented a new possibility for herself, "The possibility of being loved and cherished."

Never Too Late for Love

Beth sees that there will be a lot to learn to live inside this new possibility. After fifty years of making it on her own she is learning how to be in a healthy loving relationship.

Postscript. I received this text from her the day after she realized her teenage boyfriend had not actually betrayed her:

"I shared the revelation with (my new beau) that you helped me discover yesterday: that I caused the breakup of my high school love, that I made up that he dumped me and that I am unlovable. He hugged me and kissed me and reiterated that that is so untrue and that I am so so lovable. OMG. Thank you!"

Completing the Past

To be open to meeting new men you will need to *complete all holds on your heart from the past.* You want to be sure you have no lingering ties with any past loves. The tricky thing about ties is that they can be negative as well as positive. Anger towards a former partner will spill over and be apparent. We all know how awful it is to go on a date with someone who tells you everything that was wrong with his former partner.

Before you begin dating, do the work of cleaning up any old regrets and resentments. Clearly your former partners did not provide you with everything you wanted or fully live up to your expectations, or you would still be with them.

There are practices for completion. It helps to work with a coach or therapist to do this well. You can use the practices from the book, *Conscious Uncoupling: 5 Steps to Living Happily Even After*. Do whatever it takes so that you can be in the present moment and available to be with a new partner.

I know that recovery from a break up takes time and work. When I divorced at age fifty-seven it took a year to heal my heart – and I was working steadily at it, with world-class coaching. I knew that life was moving fast, and I did not want to spend five years on this transition. I did the work so that I could put the past in the past and move forward to new and healthier love.

I learned how to use disappointments as opportunities for learning and growth. I learned how to make new choices. For example, when three men did not pan out, just prior to meeting Marc, I didn't make it mean that there was something wrong with me, or with dating. I graduated from the old painful belief that "I am on my own" and took on the actions that matched the truth that "I am deeply connected to others" and kept reaching out to men I hadn't met yet.

In addition, while I was waiting for Marc to come, I believed that my intended was also completing things from the past so that he would be ready for a committed relationship when we met.

And that is exactly what was happening.

I met Marc just as his son was beginning a life of healthy recovery. This was the first time in many years that Marc had time and space to focus on a relationship. And I was the fortunate woman who was there at the moment when he was ready to love again!

Get complete with your past, and be confident that your intended is getting complete with his. Then you will both be available to create a life you love together.

Learn How to Have a (Real) Man in Your Life

"I Love You Just the Way You Are."
– Sung by Billy Joel

When Marc and I did finally meet, nine months after first seeing each other's profiles online, we enjoyed our conversation and were immediately attracted to each other. I tell clients to pay attention to how you *feel* when you are with a man. Yes, you will be using your brain to assess him, but this is not a job interview. You want to know how it feels for you to be with this person. You do this by keeping the focus on yourself.

Reflection Questions for Meeting a New Man:
- *Am I enjoying myself?*

- *Do I feel recognized and listened to?*
- *Do I feel comfortable?*

This is what you can learn on a first date. I felt all of these in my first meeting with Marc – enough to know that I would like to see him again.

When meeting a potential partner be sure that you are coming from the most mature and confident part of yourself – the part of you that knows your own value, the part of you that knows you do not need to rush into a relationship just to have someone by your side. You may want to know right away if this is your partner, but for most of us this will take time to find out. I went on many first, second, and third dates with men, only to learn in time that there was some way that we just did not fit.

Criteria for Choosing a Man

You have an image in your mind of the type of man you will be attracted to. Meeting many men will expand your horizons. Open yourself up to different types of men. This will allow you to learn what you are attracted to, what you don't want to be around (deal breakers), and what you can compromise on. This knowledge will refine your search.

Just before I met Marc I had the thought that what I needed for compatibility was to find someone from the same ethnic background as myself. (All four of my grandparents were immigrants from Eastern Europe and my DNA is ninety percent Eastern European Jewish, according to Ancestry.com).

I was raised with some religious education, but my life experiences were more like that of other assimilated upwardly mobile immigrant groups. And, like more than half of Jews from my generation, I had already married outside of my religion.

But in the quest to find a partner in my later years, I thought that common background might be what I needed. I dated several Jewish men, but didn't find anyone that I was drawn to.

Marc is also the grandchild of immigrants (his were French Canadian) who aspired to have their children succeed. We both had been fortunate to find careers that let us express our values. Marc shares his love for peace every day as a mediator working with families with special needs children and the schools that serve them. I have worked as a consultant who supports individuals and organizations to lead for results.

We enjoy the same kinds of friends, similar music, and spending time in nature. We have many similar interests and attitudes that allow us to live together happily. We were impressed with how each other had approached life, work, and the raising of children. We participate in many recreational activities together – the gym, yoga, walking, bicycling, and socializing. It is fun to have a partner to share these things with. We also share the commonality of having had fathers who were hard-working, high-functioning alcoholics, and we attend Al-Anon together.

I tell my clients, don't go into dating with rigid preconceived notions of what your partner will be like. You have a vision of what it will feel like to be in a beautiful relationship, but don't limit yourself to a list of characteristics of a perfect husband. You might be surprised by the kind of man you enjoy being with at this stage of life.

Take Time Getting to Know Each Other. Marc took the slow route in getting to know me. The first three months we actually did "go out." We went out to eat, out to museums, out to movies, out for walks in the woods, and out to meet friends.

His not asking me to have sex in the first three months as we were getting to know each other served us well to establish a strong foundation of friendship and caring for each other before becoming physically intimate. I highly recommend waiting before going to bed together, and also discussing why you want to wait.

Ideals Versus Values

Six months into our relationship, I attended a service for the Jewish New Year. This is a sentimental holiday for me and reminds me of my parents and my roots. Marc was happy to support me in this, and even came with me to the service. But he wanted to know, in no uncertain terms, if not being Jewish was going to be a deal breaker for me. He had previously dated a woman who would not bring him home to meet her family because he wasn't Jewish.

This was a big question that touched at the core of my values. I had an ideal of someone who came from a common ethnic background, but Marc and I shared many core values. I wasn't ready to choose him as a life partner yet, but at the same time, I wasn't ready to ask this wonderful man to leave my life because he wasn't Jewish. I made a choice. I told him it would not be a deal breaker, and I would not raise it again. I have stuck to that choice and I am forever grateful that I did.

Be clear about your values, but leave your heart open to a person who may not fit all your ideal criteria. Love in your later years can be eye opening. Enjoy your partner with all the varied experiences and background he brings to the relationship.

Reflection Questions for Beginning a Relationship:
- *How do you feel when you are with this man?*
- *What commonalities will make living a life together easier?*
- *What values do you share?*

Choosing This Man
About a year into our relationship there was a day when I couldn't find Marc for about four hours and I got scared. In my fear that something had happened to him,

I realized I didn't want to lose all the love that this man had brought into my life. I felt how important he was to me. I was enormously relieved when I learned that he had been in a long dental appointment and couldn't answer his phone!

In Marc I had found someone who could appreciate me. He appreciated that I had been a single mother and he knew what that had entailed. He had been a single father and had raised his first son alone for seven years. He had worked hard to make his career as a mediator work, and recognized that I had worked hard to become a successful organizational consultant.

We shared the same work and family values. We were both proud of how our children had turned out and of our work accomplishments. We were both sorry that our first families had not endured as originally hoped.

Committing

It takes time to learn if someone is your life's partner. I once heard Ann Landers, the newspaper advice columnist, speak about how to choose a marital partner. She suggested taking at least two years before deciding to commit to marriage. She said that over a two-year period you would have many opportunities to see how a person responds in a variety of situations. This was brilliant advice that I found to be true.

Reflection Questions When Choosing a Potential Partner:
- *Do you feel cherished and valued when you are with him?*
- *Do you share a common set of values?*
- *How does he treat his family and friends?*
- *Do you like sharing him with others in your life?*
- *How does he handle money?*
- *How does he handle disappointments?*
- *Do you encourage each other to be your best and to move forward in your lives?*

Most importantly does he treat you as a priority in his life? You don't want to play second fiddle to anyone.

Only by taking the time to learn the answers to these questions can you make a real choice about a life partner. The moment came for me two years into our relationship when we were in a Landmark Education Communications Course. In the course I had a deep insight that, due to events in my early years, I had taken on a very young belief that, "Men can't be trusted."

As this belief surfaced to consciousness, I looked over at Marc sitting next to me and saw that this was a very trustworthy man. He had proven this to me over the course of two years through many situations.

Marc had asked me to marry him prior to this. He believes that if he loves a woman he should commit to her fully. I was the one who had been hesitant about committing.

As my mind cleared, I saw this good man sitting next to me, and I leaned over to him and whispered, "Why don't you propose to me again?" Marc immediately said, "Will you marry me?"

I said, "Yes."

And the rest is our "happily ever after."

I wish you your own "*happily ever after.*"

Living Happily Ever After

"Is this the little girl I carried, is this the little boy at play, I don't remember growing older, when did they?"
– Sunrise, Sunset from Fiddler on the Roof

Marc and I have created a life together that neither of us could have created alone. We invited only our children, our siblings and their families to our intimate family wedding. Marc's sister and daughter escorted him down the "aisle." My brother and son escorted me. We truly felt "held" by our families."

We walked to the ironic words of *Sunrise, Sunset* from *Fiddler on the Roof*: "Is this the little girl I carried, is this the little boy at play, I don't remember growing older, when did they?" Marc and I were the ones who hadn't remembered growing older!

We wrote a marriage covenant to each other that we read aloud. Marc's oldest son Aaron and my daughter Rebecca signed as witnesses.

Our marriage covenant reads:

From this day forward, we will share and uphold these promises, to ensure that our marriage is blessed with abundance, health, and happiness.

As we embark on life's journey, we promise to love, cherish, encourage and inspire one another, and to be faithful, compassionate and kind.

We pledge to nurture and trust each other throughout our married life together. To respect each other's needs and help fulfill each other's dreams.

We promise to celebrate life's joys with grace, and to comfort one another through life's sorrows.

May we maintain the intimacy that fosters trust, honesty, and communication.

We choose each other as friends according to the teachings of our ancestors who said, "Acquire a friend with whom you will learn, next to whom you will sleep, and in whom you will confide."

We take on all the duties and rights of family members toward each other.

Together, we shall create a home filled with learning, laughter and compassion, a home wherein we will honor each other's cherished family traditions and values.

We promise to lead a life of justice and loving kindness in our family and in our communities. Let us join hands to help build a world filled with peace and love.

May we continue to grow together, maintaining the courage and determination to pursue our dreams and live full contributing lives.

Through each other's eyes, we see the world anew: may we be better together.

All this is valid and binding.

We are living these vows in our life today.

We concluded the ceremony by kissing every one of our relatives, including our youngest son Eli's and his girlfriend Meg's Golden Retriever puppy.

Building a Life Together

The line that I remember the most from our covenant is, "Acquire a friend with whom you will learn, next to whom you will sleep, and in whom you will confide." This describes our life together well. We experience the joy that comes from a shared and mutually caring life.

He's Not You!

A client asked me the other day if you would ever get annoyed with someone who was the right match for you. I told her, "On a daily basis!" He's not you; he's a different person with a different background, experiences, and points of view. He doesn't do things the way you would do them, because he doesn't think the way you think. This doesn't make him wrong, just different, and occasionally annoying.

You can live alone and have everything go exactly the way you want. Or you can live with a loving partner and learn how to accept someone else's ways – this is your choice. If you pick a good and loving man, as I have, it's not a hard decision. Marc always wants to do things that work for both of us. We have learned together how to be happy and contented. It feels like we are growing up at last. We both had to do a lot of inner work to get to this point.

I got more than I bargained for: not only a kind man to love and share my life with, but also a large group of beautiful young people to care about – our seven children and their partners. I could not have asked for more!

I believe that you can have this great joy in your life.

Vision of Family Love Fulfilled

When Marc and I decided to get married, I created a *Vision of Family Love Fulfilled* that we are living in now:

Relaxation and joy
Smiling, watching the children play
Deeply satisfied and proud
This is the life, the love, the family that
I've always wanted.
A big loving family spending time together happily
I feel happy, loving, secure
I contribute my family's welcoming love to him,
and feel proud of this
I receive his nectar, his heart, affection,
and his sole commitment
I feel like a light beaming to heaven.
Ecstatic!
The circle of care – all in – one family –
caring and connected.
We take good care of each other
We are safe and secure
We are strong and contributing as we age
I am the loving partner, the wise matriarch,
With concern for all
Connected with those I love
Gracious
Secure about the future.
Laughter, Appreciation, Acceptance

This is the family life that Marc and I live into every day.

This experience has affected me so much that I trained with Katherine Woodward Thomas and became certified as a *Calling in "The One"* coach, specializing in coaching women in the second half of life. I use all that I have learned in my career as a leadership coach, combined with the wise teachings about love from Katherine, to help women bring happy healthy love into their lives.

Have the courage to find this for yourself. It is out there if you will only commit to finding it.

Obstacles to Getting
the Love You Deserve

There are three major obstacles to dating and finding love in the second half of life: self-consciousness about your looks, fear of online dating, and fear of giving up your autonomy.

Successful women like you have faced these challenges and achieved the result they most wanted – happy healthy love in their lives. But you need to be aware of these potential roadblocks.

Self-Consciousness About Your Looks

When I divorced at fifty-seven, I was terrified. I had heard all the talk that older men preferred younger women.

I've learned that that's not true for men of substance. Yesterday, in the pool in our complex in Florida, Marc and I spent time with newlyweds, a couple in their sixties who have been married for one year.

They were happy to tell us about their grandchildren. But most touching was the way this husband looked at his bride. She, like me, did not have the body of a twenty-five-year-old. But you could tell from the look on her husband's face that this was a man who was crazy about his wife. (People often tell me that Marc looks at me this way.)

We look the way we do, and the men look the way they do. One woman I coached was worried because she didn't find older men attractive. My advice: find one that you do think is attractive!

I think my husband is very attractive, and he feels the same way about me. Despite our wrinkles and the persistent "love handles" around our waists, we both always love to get into bed with each other. Marc tells me I am beautiful, and the more often he tells me, the more I feel it.

I feel prettier now than I did in any other decade of my life. But it took a bit to get here. When I first decided to do online dating I focused on losing weight. (I've focused on losing weight throughout my life, and I am still at least thirty pounds overweight!)

Fortunately Marc was not looking for a thin woman. All of the extra softness that I carry on my body is attractive to my husband. He would hug me all the time if I let him. We look like a couple who are well suited to each other.

I knew that I was beginning to overcome my body insecurities in the second year of dating, when I asked someone to join me for a second date at the beach. Despite a second date in a bathing suit, I was asked out for a third date, at which time we both realized that we weren't compatible for other reasons.

Many women in their later years who look their age have found love. If you need help with your confidence about your looks, reach out to get the support you need to overcome your insecurities. You can do this!

Fear of Online Dating

I've given you all of the tips you need to successfully date online. But I can understand that this can be daunting if you have never done it before, or if you have put your toe in the water only to dredge up a few frogs.

I told you about Sue, who was divorced at age sixty after a thirty-eight-year marriage to someone she had met in high school. She was terrified of online dating. Would the men expect her to have sex? And when she did go online, it was equally terrifying: *People she liked didn't respond to her, and people who responded to her weren't great matches.*

It wasn't until she learned how set up a good profile and how to reach out to men online that she started to have any success. Now she is seventy and in a happy relationship with a man, enjoying their mature acceptance of who they both are. She encourages other women to go online, but she warns them, "Get a coach if you don't want to get discouraged!"

The man of your dreams is most likely not going to drop through your ceiling, ring your doorbell, or sit next to you at a luncheon. If you want to discover someone you can be compatible with, you're going to have to meet available men. And online dating sites offer the largest number of potential partners.

Even if you have the means, as one of my clients did, to use a matchmaking service, this is still no guarantee that you will meet the man you can be compatible with. My client Emily paid a matchmaker a good amount of money to come up with a few "men of means," only to find out they many of them were looking for a woman to act as a support system for them.

She ran back to online dating where men of lesser means were looking for equal partners in life.

There are a million reasons not to go on online dating sites. But unfortunately, this is the one place where there is a volume of men who have declared that they are 1) available, and 2) interested in having a relationship. Just by using a dating site, you have already screened men for these two criteria. It is up to you to sort them for what you most care about.

You can learn how to use these sites. You can do this!

You Fear Giving up Your Autonomy

You have worked hard to create the life you have. I know what this means to you. By time I was in my late fifties I had enough of a reputation in the world of leadership development that I could work for myself and determine my own fees and my own hours.

My parents raised me to be confident. I've had enough education and experiences to make my own judgments about things, and I enjoy using my mind to address complex challenges. I am not someone who needs to be told what to do. In fact, I bristle a bit when people try to tell me what to do!

Do I "need" a man? No. I could survive perfectly well without one for the rest of my life. But do I want to share my life with a man? Yes, very much so.

This is the question that you must answer for yourself: *Are you better off alone - or would you like to reach out to see what closeness and intimacy would be like at this stage of your life?*

Living with a man will require you to be responsive to another's needs and preferences. But I want you to know that if you find a good and kind man who truly loves you, he will respect your autonomy. He will support the decisions you make in your life – as long as he knows that he is included in your decision-making.

This past fall I went to a nine-day leadership program in Mexico. My first teacher in leadership, Werner Erhard, was giving the course, and my current mentor and friend, Katherine Woodward Thomas, was inviting me to attend with her.

Marc and I were driving in the car when I learned about the course. As soon as he heard the details, he told me, "You have to go!" I registered for the course before we even got home. Marc always wants to support me, even though he misses me terribly when I'm away.

I am someone who held a strong belief that, "I have to make it on my own." This belief gave me a good life in many ways. I learned how find a career that I loved and could earn good money from. I raised my children and helped them with college and graduate school. And I formed supportive friendships with people I respect and care for.

But this does not compare to what it's like to have a kind and loving partner in my life. Living with Marc, being married to him, sharing our families with each other – these are the crowning glories of my life. Marc and I say, that after a long life of many challenges, we won – we found love!

If you are afraid that having a man in your life will limit you in some ways, please reach out to a good coach or therapist and get clear about your choice.

If you do choose to find love, I believe you will find that it will be worth the tradeoffs.

Conclusion:

Love Is Waiting for You

"I could make you happy, make your dreams come true. Nothing that I wouldn't do. Go to the ends of the earth for you, to make you feel my love."
–Bob Dylan

I wrote this book because I want the single women in my generation to know that there is a way to find happy, healthy love. I want to help you to face the challenges of online dating, and get the support you need to persevere in the face of the inevitable disappointments.

You are not alone. Our generation is learning how to pair-bond in new ways, and at later stages of life. There are ways to do this and there are practices you need to learn to be successful. These practices are:

1. **Clarify your intention**. Be clear about the love you are intending to create, and share your intention with a committed listener or a coach to sustain yourself on the path to getting the love you deserve.

2. **Envision love fulfilled.** Use all of your senses to create, in the present moment, the experience of love that you are intending to create. Learn how to *be* the experience that you want to have.

3. **Learn how to date online.** Set up a profile, get the right photos, and learn how to respond to men online. Learn how to keep going, even in the face of setbacks.

4. **Learn to deal with the disappointments of online dating.** Uplevel your old false beliefs to formulate more powerful ones that reflect a truer view of reality – *that you are valuable, and that you do have a right to be loved and cherished!*

5. **Open your life to having a real man.** A good and kind man who will love you, although he may not be to your exact order. Learn what is really important to you in a partner at this stage of your life.

My hope for you is that you use these practices to bring love into your life. I am committed to supporting you to find this love.

Many of these practices will take you out of your comfort zone. In fact, the biggest problem I have seen with my clients is the tendency to want to quit when the going gets tough. That's what coaching is for – to help you through the obstacles when your own thinking is not sufficient to the task. Learning to receive love in your life will require new ways of thinking.

A client recently wrote,

"It was another mind-opening coaching session with you this morning. Through talking to you about my observations of my behaviors and thoughts, you have helped me to become more aware of myself.

"More importantly, you provided guidance on how to change my subconscious thoughts and thereby my behaviors, especially those automatic/habitual behaviors I have put up to protect myself and that prevent me from truly living my life."

My hope is that reading this book has given you renewed hope and confidence to engage in the process of finding a loving partner.

Please share your progress with me. I want to hear about both your successes and your setbacks. We need to share our knowledge and encourage each other.

Because, in the end, *love is all there is.*

Recommended Sources

Readings:
Calling in "The One": 7 Weeks to Attract the Love of Your Life by Katherine Woodward Thomas

Conscious Uncoupling: 5 Steps to Living Happily Even After by Katherine Woodward Thomas

Late Love: Mating in Maturity by Avivah Wittenberg Cox

Why He Disappeared by Evan Marc Katz

Leading for Results: Five Practices to Use in Your Personal and Professional Life by Joan Bragar

Movie:
Book Club; four women in their later years bravely finding love.

Acknowledgments

Learning how to love is a lifelong process. I want to first thank my parents, Norman and Eleanor Bragar, who loved me always, and my brother Robert, who taught me, through his example, the value of committed loving relationships that last a lifetime.

My children Rebecca and Michael have been with me over the past four decades as I learned how to bring healthy love into my life. I am grateful for their patience and love.

My heartfelt thanks go to Katherine Woodward Thomas, my friend, teacher, coach, and fellow traveler on the road to love; and to the coaches in the *Calling in "The One"* community who, under Katherine's wise leadership, create a loving container for learning and growth.

Thank you to Angela Lauria and The Author Incubator's team, as well as to David Hancock and the Morgan James Publishing team for helping me bring this book to print.

Finally, and always, this is for Marc, my wonderful husband, who shows me in every moment the power of love. Thank you for sharing your life and your loving family with me.

Thank You!

Thank you so much for reading my book.

The fact that you've gotten to this point in the book tells me something important about you: *You are interested in bringing happy, healthy love into your life.*

To support you in moving forward, you can take this self-assessment,

"Am I ready for love?"

This simple assessment will help you get crystal-clear about where you are in your journey to a life of love.

You can get your copy of this at:
www.joanbragar.com

And don't hesitate to reach out to me at:
joan@joanbragar.com

About the Author

Joan Bragar, through her doctoral studies at Harvard and ongoing work, researched the practices that lead to results in all areas of life. She now focuses her work on coaching women who want to learn the practices that contribute to success in intimate relationships. She is especially effective with successful women who are high performers in other areas of life.

She learned the importance of getting support for finding love when she divorced in her late fifties. She knew that she wanted to be in a loving partnership with a man again. To heal her heart and learn the practices that would make healthy love possible, she worked with Katherine Woodward Thomas, best-selling author of *Calling in "The One"* and *Conscious Uncoupling*.

She met Marc, her beloved husband, just before her sixtieth birthday. They were married when she was sixty-two – with their seven grown children as witnesses. She then trained and was certified as a *Calling in "The One"* and *Conscious Uncoupling* coach, specializing in women in the second half of life.

Joan has worked as a professor of leadership, a management consultant, and a coach to people around the world in corporate, academic, and health care settings. She has created leadership development programs that have been offered in more than forty-five countries. Her book, *Leading for Results, Five Practices to Use in Your Personal and Professional Life*, maps out the practices you need to apply to move from vision to effective action in the areas of life that are most important to you.

Joan is now the doting matriarch of a large family that includes seven grown children and their partners, and four wonderful grandchildren. She lives with her husband Marc Sevigny in Boston and Punta Gorda, Florida.

If, after reading this book, you are interested in additional coaching, please call Joan at 857-728-4998.

You can connect with Joan at www.joanbragar.com

And you can write to her at joan@joanbragar.com

9 781642 797923